Dividend Investing Your Way to Financial Freedom

A Guide to Live Off Dividends Forever

www.MillionaireMob.com

© 2018 Millionaire Mob

All rights reserved. No portion of this book may be reproduced in any form without permission from the publisher, except as permitted by U.S. copyright law. For permissions contact:

info@millionairemob.com

ASIN: B07JFZ18VQ

ISBN: 9781728963242

Introduction

Stock markets are volatile. Global financial crises have shown they can make drastic swings in short periods. There are far too many examples of considerable volatilities in the stock market in the last few decades that resulted in the losses of billions of dollars to investors. For example, during the 2007/08 financial bubble, the U.S. stock market lost half of its value in just a few months alone. Similarly, the subsequent low-growth economy that followed the global crisis significantly impacted several companies' financial performances, share prices, and dividends. Many investors were left hanging for a long time.

However, there are plenty of investment opportunities that not only offer stable and substantial returns during the period of prosperity, but they also provide the hedge against the downturn. There are millions of ways to make money in the stock market every single day. At the same time, you need to stick to your plan for investing. The moment you stray away from what's working is the moment you get caught in a relentless financial storm that could uproot your life. To avoid a dramatic downfall, I will show you how to craft an optimal dividend portfolio and reap the benefits of investing for income without losing out on the prospects of growth.

Companies that offer a strong dividend with the long history of raising dividends at a respectable rate are popular among investors. For instance, Johnson & Johnson, 3M, and many other dividend-paying companies are among investor's favorites. These types of companies are not only financially stable, but investors also trust in their potential to generate a sustainable growth over the long-term. What if you could find the next Johnson & Johnson or 3M?

My goal is to live off of my dividends forever and I'll show you how you can too!

About the Author

Millionaire Mob is a financial freedom and early retirement blogger focused on improving lifestyles through investing, passive income, and travel.

As a former investment banker, I wanted to create something that everyone could learn from without the gimmicks offered by Wall Street. I am a true believer that dividend growth investing is the best way to build wealth through compound interest.

Over the last decade, I've invested in both private and public markets. Throughout my career, I've acquired multibillion-dollar businesses and I've also built a portfolio of stocks that have consistently outperformed the market. However, with all of my success stories, I too have had failures along the way.

Now, I want you to learn from my successes and my mistakes. I've always said the best way to learn is through your mistakes. The only better way is to learn from *someone else's* mistakes.

If you want to build true wealth over time and have your money work for you while you sleep, work, and enjoy the good things in life then I hope you'll keep reading.

Through Personal Capital net worth tracking, I was able to grow my net worth from -$60,000 (yes, that's *negative*) to over half a million dollars by focusing on my dividend growth investing strategy and increasing my overall income.

This guide is for you.

Of course, you know what they say:

"The best time to plant a tree was 20 years ago. The second-best time is now."

Table of Contents

Prologue: Resources I Love

Chapter 1: Introduction to Dividend Stocks

1.1. What Are Dividend Stocks?

1.2. Reasons for Dividend Investing

1.3. The Distinction Between Growth, Value, and Dividend Stocks

Chapter 2: Technical and Fundamental Analysis of Stock

2.1. The Importance of Technical and Fundamentals Analysis for Dividend Stock Selection

2.2. Technical Analysis

2.3. Fundamental Analysis

Chapter 3: Dividend Stock Selection Strategies

3.1. Fundamental Analysis and Strategies

3.2. Consider Companies with Long Histories and Strong Brands

3.3. The Company Must Have a Strong Competitive Advantage

3.4. Make the Long Run Strategy

3.5. Look for Shareholder-Friendly Management

3.6. Dividend Payout Ratio

3.7. Focus on Straight Forward Approach, Either a High Dividend Yield or a High Dividend Growth Rate Approach

Chapter 4: How to Find Undervalued Dividend Growth Stocks

4.1. Finding Undervalued Dividend Growth Stocks

4.2. Dividend Growth at a Reasonable Price (dGARP)

4.3. How to Screen for Undervalued Dividend Growth Stocks (Infographic)

4.4. Compare Dividend Growth Screener Results with Dividend Aristocrats Index

Chapter 5: Dividend Discount Model

5.1. What Is the Dividend Discount Model?

5.2. Short-Form Dividend Discount Model

5.3. Multi-Stage Dividend Discount Model

5.4. Problems with Using the Dividend Discount Model

5.5. What Is the Gordon Growth Model or Short-Form Dividend Discount Model?

Chapter 6: Dividend Growth Rate Forecast Methods

6.1. How to Forecast the Dividend Growth Rate?

6.2. What Other Considerations Are Needed for Dividend Growth Investing?

6.3. Expert Opinion on How to Forecast Dividend Growth Rate

Chapter 7: The Role of Technical Analysis in Stock Selection

7.1. The Importance of Technical Analysis

7.2. The Importance of Moving Average and How to Use a Moving Average to Buy Stocks

7.3. Why Use a Moving Average?

7.4. Types of Moving Averages

7.5. Candlestick Patterns

Chapter 8: How to Improve Income Through Smart Strategies

8.1. How to Pick a Technically and Fundamentally Sound Stock for Dividend Portfolio

8.2. Income Generation Through Binary Trading

8.3. What Are Covered Calls?

8.4. Example of Writing Covered Calls with Dividend Growth Stocks

8.5. Best Stocks for Covered Call Writing

8.6. What Are Put Options?

8.7. Writing Puts for Income Checklist

8.8. What Are the Stock Long-Term Fundamentals?

8.9. What Are Material Events Happening Between Now and Expiration of the Weekly Put Option?

Chapter 9: Which Sectors Offer Best Dividends?

9.1. Where to Look for Dividend Stocks

Chapter 10: The Theoretical Case Against Dividend Investing

10.1. The Case Against High Dividend Yields

10.2. Dividend Growers as a Quality Proxy

10.3. A Note on Dividend Growth Portfolios

10.4. Dividends Are Not Legally Binding

Conclusion

Appendix: Free Downloadable Resources

Resources I Love

Here are some of my favorite resources that have helped me become a better dividend growth investor.

I believe these resources are **must-haves** for any aspiring or experienced dividend investor. These resources have helped me build my wealth from -$60,000 to nearly half a million in just five years. If you want to be a successful investor, you must arm yourself with the best financial tools in the business. Just like in business, you need to invest money in the tools that help you grow to truly succeed.

I know that if I'm going to invest thousands of dollars over a long period of time, I am very comfortable paying for premium services to empower myself to succeed. It's all about **working smarter, not harder.** These resources will help you achieve financial success.

1. FINVIZ

FINVIZ is absolutely necessary if you want to screen for undervalued dividend stocks. I use FINVIZ *every single day* to generate new investment ideas, monitor my existing portfolio, and more. Here is how I use FINVIZ Elite to understand market trends. If you have never used FINVIZ, here is how to use FINVIZ to screen for stocks.
Join FINVIZ Elite to generate new investment ideas instantly.

2. Robinhood Investing App

I've been using Robinhood to build a dividend portfolio from scratch. You can even follow along with my Robinhood dividend investing portfolio updates. I'd love to show you that anyone can build wealth through dividend growth investing.

If you join Robinhood, we both get a share of free stock!

3. GuruFocus

GuruFocus is an under-the-radar investing website. As with FINVIZ, I use GuruFocus to generate new investment ideas. The name GuruFocus originates from the company's focus on following several high-profile investment pros, including Warren Buffett, Seth Klarman, David Einhorn, and more. This is invaluable to me because I love following investors who influenced me to get started.

Join GuruFocus Pro to follow Warren Buffett's investment criteria and more. If you join with my link, you'll get a free month of pro-access!

4. Investopedia

If you want to become more familiar with the ins and outs of trading and investing, Investopedia is a great resource for you. Their trading academy can help you make money overnight!

Join Investopedia and start making money in the stock market today!

5. Personal Capital

I owe much of my success to Personal Capital. They have an amazing net worth tracking and investment allocation section of the platform. It is completely free to use and tracks budgeting in addition to your investment accounts. I'm grateful for their dashboard and amazing customer support.

Join Personal Capital with my link and get a FREE investment consultation.

Chapter One: Introduction to Dividend Stocks

1.1. What Are Dividend Stocks?

There are few companies that offer dividends. Financially stable and strong companies usually offer a dividend as a sign of gratitude to their shareholders. On the other hand, companies in the process of expanding their businesses usually reinvest their profits in future growth opportunities rather than paying dividends to investors.

When an investor buys a stock of a dividend paying company, the investor is entitled to get the share portion of profit according to its ownership. Dividends are distributed on a per share basis. For instance, if you own 100 shares of XYZ Company, these 100 shares serve as the basis of your dividends. You bought these 100 shares at $100 per share, so you've invested a total amount of $10,000. The Board of Directors approves to pay the dividend of $1 per share on an annual basis. This means that you will get $100 on an annual basis in dividends.

The Distribution of Profit Among the Shareholders Is Called a Dividend.

Typically, only a certain portion of companies pay dividends. These companies have established business models along with the confidence in their future fundamentals. The top managerial staff decides (and the Board of Directors approve) whether they will distribute their profit to shareholders in the form of dividends, or if they will reinvest those earnings back into the company. Dividends are paid on a monthly, quarterly, or annual basis.

Dividend Yield

Believe it or not, new investors often believe that a higher stock price means higher dividends. In reality, when the stock price increases, it generally has a negative impact on the dividend yield. The dividend yield declines with the growth in share price.

So, how can you figure out the dividend yield? It's easy! Simply divide the number of dividends paid to you ($100) by the amount you have invested in the stock ($10,000). After dividing these figures, you will come up with a dividend yield of 1%. You can't always rely on dividend yield when investing.

1.2. Reasons for Dividend Investing

Dividend investing is popular because investors like to receive a steady stream of income in the form of dividends. Typically, these companies have strong business models. They may have some of the most outstanding reputations in the industry and their stock performance reflects that. Furthermore, these entrenched organizations frequently raise dividends every year. For instance, 3M has increased its dividends each year for more than 50 consecutive years.

Given that the majority of dividend-paying stocks are less exposed to market volatility due to their stable business model and cash flow generation potential, they are a favorite among both experienced retail investors as well as institutional investors.

There are many reasons that dividend stocks tend to do better than their counterparts. Let's look at each.

Historical Data

Dividend stocks are deemed as a cushion against a volatile business environment. Although past performances never indicate future prospects, dividend stocks have overperformed the Standard & Poor's 500-stock index returns over the decades. Since 1960, nearly 30% of S&P 500 overall returns arrived from dividend stocks.

Based on RBC Global Asset Management research, dividend stocks have generated 11.7% compounded annual returns over the last three decades. A Hartford Funds white paper also found that, since 1960, nearly 81% of S&P 500 returns can be ascribed to reinvested dividends, thanks to the power of compounding. That is powerful.

Compounding Makes Dividends Extremely Attractive

The power of compounding really works for dividend investors. When dividend investors reinvest dividends to buy additional shares, which results in higher dividends, the dividend compounding phenomenon occurs.

Several dividend reinvestment plans are available for investors to buy additional shares of a company without paying any commission on top of the share price. In some cases, companies offer their shares at a discount to investors according to their dividend reinvestment plan ("DRIP"). Your returns become quite attractive when you don't have to pay a fee for purchasing only a handful of shares.

From the organization's angle, DRIPs might be appealing in light of the fact that the DRIP shares can be sold in a simple manner by the organization. Dividend reinvestment can allow organizations to raise a new capital to spur growth or allow for liquidity for existing shareholders. There's a value proposition for both angles.

Dividend reinvestment allows investors to expand their overall returns over the longer-term. For instance, if a person invests $5000 in the company at a share price of $50 while the company offers a dividend of 2.5%, the investor will receive $125 in dividends at the end of the first year. These dividends lead to an overall investment increase of $5,125. Now, let's suppose the company has a policy to increase the dividend by 5% each year and the investors have reinvested all of the dividends. After 20 years, the investor's total investment would be valued at over $11,000, excluding the share price change.

Higher Earnings Quality

Accounting is all about estimates and assumptions. Several companies and businesses have recently attempted to show elevated earnings and estimates. They can do this easily. *How?* A number of companies can do this by making a select few changes to their depreciation methods. It's actually quite easy for management to present higher income figures and assumptions compared to actual figures which may be lower.

Typically, companies have been working on these behaviors to give a temporary boost to the share price and traders confidence. Investors and traders should know a bit about forensic accounting to detect these techniques.

However, in the case of dividend-paying companies, the chance of presenting misleading figures is very low. The management cannot fake investors on the real cash. Real cash doesn't include non-cash items, reducing the management's potential to present higher figures. Thus, investing in companies that have a long dividend history and continually increase their dividend payouts are the real cash-making machines.

Dividend Yields Are Hedge Against Market Break Down

Although value investing has the potential to offer bigger returns to investors in the case of price appreciation, they also have the potential to create big losses for investors during the major meltdowns. During periods of depression, dividend-paying stocks remain stronger than non-dividend stocks. Dividend-paying companies usually have strong balance sheets, and their business models are more stable to cope with the market downturn.

Let's create a demo portfolio to see how the market changes impacts a company's performance and shareholder value. Suppose an investor has invested $100,000 into two stocks: Berkshire Hathaway and Johnson & Johnson. The investor has invested $50,000 in each. Additionally, let's imagine the investor hasn't been managing the portfolio well.

Since 1960, Berkshire Hathaway hasn't paid a dividend. On the other hand, Johnson & Johnson has a long dividend history and it has increased its dividends every year in the last three decades. Even the 2007/08 global financial crisis couldn't stop the company from raising its dividends. Plus, the company's share prices stood taller in front of headwinds, thanks to its stable balance sheet and cash position.

Let's imagine the market plunges and stocks lost almost half of their original values. This means that the portfolio worth $100,000 has declined to $50,000 in just a single day, resulting in a loss of $50,000 to investors from both stocks. Despite the selloff in share price, JNJ sends you a dividend check each quarter. Moreover, with the decline in the share price, JNJ's dividend yield will double. The dividend will also help the investors to put a floor under the stock price and stabilize it.

Human instinct also prefers to keep those investments that offer regular checks with a steady appreciation of initial investment. Investors prefer to hold investments in stocks that offer strong resistance against the market volatility. In addition, regular dividends are extremely appealing; mainly the markets are going to face enormously complicated business conditions.

Disciplined in Capital Investing

The management of dividend-paying companies generally needs to be more disciplined in their cash management. These companies distribute their cash flows in the way that they can sustain gradual sales and earnings growth along with returning cash to investors. If the CEO finds two potential acquisitions opportunities, he suddenly needs to pick the more lucrative alternative with the better guarantee of extending benefits.

The dividend has a huge impact on the share price performance of any stock. The dividend payments and the growth in dividends in particular move share prices higher. In addition, stock prices of companies with a history of raising dividends at a respectable rate stand taller against the market volatilities and their stable business models offer a hedge against market volatilities.

It makes sense that the likelihood of making a steady stream of income through investing in dividend stocks or holding that stock over the long-term encourages share prices of these companies. While this inspiration may appear to be simply temperate, the fundamental convictions about the organization's earnings are what affect shares the most.

1.3. The Distinction Between Growth, Value, and Dividend Stocks

Generally, investors look to buy stocks for two major reasons: they expect to get a dividend from the company against their investment, or they believe their investment will increase in the form of share price appreciation. There's no doubt that a few stocks can please investors with both dividend and value to some degree. However, the majority of stocks are categorized as such: income, growth, or value.

Growth Stocks

Growth stocks, as the name suggests, are those companies that have the generous potential for development within a reasonable time-frame. Growth companies try to expand their business at a higher rate and they reinvest all of their profits back into the business. We can find growth companies in every sector; however, they are more likely to be found in energy, technology, and biotechnology.

The majority of growth stocks are generally new in the market and the returns from these companies rely entirely on how they will perform in the future.

Let's take an example of Starbucks (Nasdaq: SBUX) as a growth stock. This company, which is in the process of establishing its footprints, shows considerable growth potential in global markets. The company is planning to expand its presence in the Chinese markets along with other Asian countries. The company also plans to open new shops in America and it is planning to expand in Europe as well.

Value Stocks

Value investors look to create value by investing in stocks that are undervalued. These undervalued stocks have the potential to generate higher returns for investors in the future. In fact, underestimated organizations can provide big gains to traders. It's difficult to find stocks that are trading below their real value, but traders can use certain ratios and calculations that suggest how undervalued a stock actually is.

For example, investors can use price-to-earnings and price-to-sales ratios. The lower ratio compared to the industry average represents a stock that is undervalued. On the other hand, higher ratios show a stock that is overvalued. In addition to these ratios, investors are encouraged to focus on the future prospects of the stock to predict the upside potential.

Dividend Stocks

Defensive investors look to buy stocks that have the potential to generate sustainable returns over the long-term. These investors buy stocks with a high dividend yield and long dividend histories. Income stocks are generally stable in nature, and the management also shows strong discipline in their capital spending. These companies have stable business models and they try to generate strong cash flows over the long-term.

Income-oriented stocks have a tendency to be among the most predictable of all stocks; in fact, many see them as a hedge against the market volatility. These stocks usually operate in the less competitive environment and they hold a steady demand despite any economic downturns.

Food, drink, and service organizations are awesome cases of defensive stocks. Even when the economy is encountering intense circumstances, people still need to eat, drink, and turn on the lights. Organizations that offer moderately high profits likewise have a tendency to be part of these more stable industries.

Usually, utilities and consumer discretionary companies are considered the best income stocks due to their potential to generate stable earnings and cash flows over the long run. These income stocks not only offer dividends, but their share prices also have the potential to move steadily in an upward trend. Investors can find several strong stocks that have the long history of returning significant cash to investors.

There are many good companies that pay great dividends and also grow at respectable rates. For instance, Johnson & Johnson has paid increasing dividends over the last several decades, and its share price has also steadily increased. The company has recently increased its dividend for the 55th straight year. The company currently offers a quarterly dividend of 0.84 per share, yielding close to 3%.

The importance of dividends has recently been forcing historically low-yield industries to return cash through dividends to investors. In the 1990's, dividends were strong in only slow-moving industries where competition was low and the barrier to entry was very high, such as utilities. However, tech stocks today, which were deemed to be a place for value investors, have turned out to be the second-biggest provider of overall dividends.

Chapter 2: Technical and Fundamental Analysis of Stock

2.1. The Importance of Technical and Fundamentals Analysis for Dividend Stock Selection

Warren Buffett, the master of dividend investing, solidly trusts in taking the long-view with regards to dividend investing. In fact, he believes that investors should know when to buy, hold, and sell a stock.

Dividend investors often fall in love with stocks and hold onto them for a longer time. It's also vital to understand the better entry points in the stocks. Buying stocks when they are undervalued and selling them on the high is a great strategy to maximize your returns.

According to Benjamin Graham's long-term value investing strategy, the key is to buy stocks below their intrinsic value and hold onto them until they've hit their real value.

Warren Buffett also loves to buy undervalued stocks of well-established companies that have a strong history of returning significant cash to investors. Buffett holds onto these stocks, enjoying their dividends. When he feels the stock has appreciated significantly, he sells it to enjoy the price appreciation.

In order to make a perfect buying decision like big business magnates, investors should have the potential to do both technical and fundamental analysis. Investors cannot understand the best buying and selling opportunities unless they have a strong hold over technical and fundamentals.

2.2 Technical Analysis

Technical analysis is a methodology used to analyze a stock's future performance by evaluating past price performances, ratios, valuations, and shares price trends. Technical analysts strongly believe that past performances and price trends are the best indicators to predict the future potential.

Dow Theory has introduced technical analysis for the first time. According to Dow Theory, technical analysis is built on two assumptions:

1. Market price discounts every factor that may influence a security's price.
2. Market price movements are not purely random but move in identifiable patterns and trends that repeat over time.

Technical analysis is important as several technical indicators rightly pick the future stock price performance. Investors can make technical analysis of any instrument whose price movement is dependent on supply and demand forces. Stock, bond, currency pairs, indices, and other securities performances are highly dependent on supply and demand.

Analysts and investors have developed several technical indicators to gauge future performances. However, every indicator has its own importance according to the market trends and price movements. A few of them are significantly focused on predicting the existing market trend. Some of the popular current market indicators are resistance and support areas. Technical analysis helps in determining the potential movements in prices. These indicators include moving averages, trendlines, and MACD indicators.

2.3 Fundamental Analysis

On the other hand, fundamental analysis is quite different from technical analysis. Fundamental analysis depends mainly on factors like economic indicators, financial numbers, and qualitative and quantitative factors. An analyst can use these tools to measure the intrinsic value of a stock. Fundamental analysis also helps investors calculate the future growth potential.

Moreover, fundamental analysis is based on real financial numbers, economic reports, and important ratios. It's not necessary that investors can only do the fundamental analysis of the stocks; they can also make a fundamental analysis of any type of security, including bonds. However, in order to evaluate stocks value and future potential, analysts mainly use figures such as earnings, revenues, future growth, profit margins, stock investment strategies, return on equity, and other data to establish a company's real price. Warren Buffett is among those investors who are well known for perfectly applying fundamental analysis to their stock selection.

For instance, Warren Buffett has recently sold one-third of his stake in **International Business Machine** (IBM), as he sees the stock has bleak future fundamentals to support the share price movement and dividends.

However, he still holds 50 million IBM shares, as the stock still looks undervalued according to major technical indicators. Strong market competition, the arrival of competing technologies, and mass level of restructuring are the major reasons behind the bleak future fundamentals of IBM.

Chapter 3: Dividend Stock Selection Strategies

3.1. Fundamental Analysis and Strategies

Fundamental analysis plays a key role in maximizing profits and minimizing risks for dividend stock portfolios. Fundamental analysis is easier than technical analysis because investors just need to understand the prospects of the industry in which the company is operating. If the investor doesn't understand the dynamics of the industry in which the stock is operating, he might not have the potential to generate high returns from stock. There are several examples where investors would have made big profits just by holding a strong grip in analyzing business dynamics.

For instance, **Caterpillar** (CAT), the largest machinery maker, experienced significant volatility in 2015 to the middle of 2016. But investors, with strong skills to understand the industry dynamics and business prospects of CAT, have generated big profits by buying the stock during the downtime.

After trading in the range of $90 to $110 per share between 2013 and 2015, its shares plunged massively in the second half of 2015 and hit the lowest level of $59 per share at the beginning of FY2016. Everything was quite predictable for investors who were sound in making a fundamental analysis.

In 2016, commodity prices were under pressure, thus demand from these industries for CAT's machinery and other products declined, eventually impacting CAT's financial numbers and share prices. However, the stock has been making a massive rebound since the start of the second half of 2016, thanks to improvement in demand from end markets.

Moreover, Caterpillar fulfills all requirements to be part of the dividend investor's portfolio, thanks to its extensive dividend history, low payout ratio, strong dividend yield, and potential to generate increasing cash flows. Caterpillar has paid a cash dividend every year since the company was formed and has paid a quarterly dividend since the 1930's.

However, buying a company's stock only due to the sharp decline in the share price is never a wise investment strategy for investors. Investors should look at various fundamental metrics before deciding to buy any stock for his or her dividend portfolio.

Remember, examining fundamentals is vital before buying any stock for the dividend portfolio. Below are a few important fundamental strategies that investors should consider when creating the perfect dividend portfolio.

3.2. Consider Companies with Long Histories and Strong Brands

Buffett puts resources into organizations with long business histories. For instance, his top five holdings have a history of more than 100 years. American Express, Wells Fargo, and Coca-Cola were all founded in the 1800s.

Organizations with long histories don't offer as many surprises as new companies do. They have established business policies and strong balance sheets and their management team knows exactly what to do and how to do it well. It's quite hard for a company to be so effective over a long period of time, due to the constantly changing business environment and technological innovations.

To prosper for a long time, these companies work on the policies that allow them to make changes in their business models according to the current business environment.

If we closely take a look at Buffett's best five positions, four out of the five are operating in slow-changing industries. Stable companies with a long history have the potential to generate strong cash flows over the long-term. In addition, operating in a slowly changing environment helps companies to make fewer investments in growth opportunities, allowing them to generate stronger returns for investors.

3.3. The Company Must Have a Strong Competitive Advantage

It is very important for investors to pick companies that have potential to expand their product portfolio according to the market requirements. Choosing a company with an enticing management team would allow it to capitalize on its market share over the long-term. Strong brand recognition is among many factors that investors should look for prior to investing in a company.

Let's draw an example to gauge why the competitive advantage is important to consider:

BlackBerry (BBRY) is among the companies whose share prices took a steep drop over a short period of time. In fact, BBRY's share price dropped from $200 to $10 in just two years. The reason for this drop is that BlackBerry failed to lure its customers in according to the market trends. Apple, Samsung, and others have snatched BlackBerry's market share in a relatively short amount of time.

However, it's also important for the long-term dividend investors to find the business with a long-term competitive advantage. For instance, we have been witnessing significant changes in the technology industry on a daily basis. Several new companies arrived in the tech industry, but **Microsoft** (MSFT) denied leaving its market share, due to its potential to timely adopt the market trends.

3.4. Make the Long Run Strategy

If you have patience and plans to spend the life on returns from your stock portfolio, you should look for longevity in the companies in which you invest. Dividend investors must hold the stock for a long time to maximize its profits.

At the beginning of this book, I used 3M as an example because it has generated dividend growth for more than 55 straight years and its share price has also appreciated massively. Let's take a look at one more dividend aristocrat to see how holding these types of stocks for the long-term can have a positive impact on overall returns.

Coca-Cola has been paying an increasing dividend over the last few decades, and its share price rose steadily during these periods.

If you want to enjoy the power of compounding, and buying and holding stocks, such companies would generate massive returns. There is also a tax advantage when you are buying and holding for a long time. At the point when you sell the stock, you are liable to pay capital tax. This is one of the essential purposes for dividend investors to buy and hold for the long-term. Moreover, more and more changes in a stock portfolio incredibly diminish portfolio turnover.

3.5. Look for Shareholder-Friendly Management

Traders cannot make profits by investing in any company unless their management is shareholder friendly. The management holds the authority on how to use their profits and cash flows. They have the authority to reinvest the entire profits or distribute them to investors. Usually, a stable company with a long, established history will distribute 30% to 50% of their cash to investors in the form of dividends. The company will then reinvest the remaining profits back into the business.

If the management is shareholder friendly, then they are probably used to being very disciplined in their capital allocation strategies. For instance, the management of Philip Morris is deemed to be user-friendly, and they have shown significant discipline in capital investments and shareholders returns. They have a long dividend history, and the management has also been returning massive cash in the form of share buybacks. However, it doesn't mean that they are not investing in future growth opportunities.

Philip Morris management knows how important its dividends are to investors. They continue to keep their dividend yield around 5% and they have recently played a smart move. Along with internal cash generation, they have borrowed money from financial markets and used those funds to reduce the outstanding shares. The lower number of outstanding shares means that the company must distribute the dividend to fewer shareholders. This way they have reduced their cash flow obligations while simultaneously increasing the value of each share.

3.6. Dividend Payout Ratio

The safety of dividends should be on the top of the investor's priority list when selecting dividend stocks for a portfolio. The safety of dividends can usually be measured by its coverage ratio. Analysts recommend investors to select stocks with a payout ratio ranging from 30% to 50%.

If a company makes a profit of $100 million, they can easily distribute dividends amounting to $30 to $50 million. In addition, these dividend paying companies create their business strategies to generate sustainable growth in revenues and earnings. Therefore, traders can expect to receive a higher dividend year after year without experiencing any change in the payout ratio.

On the other hand, several companies also keep their payout ratio in the range of 90% of their income. However, these companies have lowered the cushion against the market uncertainties. If the market uncertainty pushes the company's earnings down by 10% to 20%, it would be difficult for the management to hold dividends. U.S. energy companies are perfect examples of higher payout ratios. However, these companies have had to slash their dividends by more than 60% in 2016 following the slump in oil prices.

3.7. Focus on Straight Forward Approach, Either a High Dividend Yield or a High Dividend Growth Rate Approach

After checking the safety of dividends, investors need to choose from high dividend growth stocks or high dividend yield stocks. Both dividend stocks play a different role in various portfolios and have their particular followers. Companies that offer high dividend yields usually have stable business models and they are disciplined enough in their capital investments to keep things in order. On the other hand, high dividend growth companies always need to produce higher earnings and cash flows to distribute higher dividends year after year.

Obviously, in special circumstances, investors can get both a high dividend growth and a high dividend yield. This is the reason some asset management companies specialize in dividend investing strategies.

Chapter 4: How to Find Undervalued Dividend Growth Stocks

4.1. Finding Undervalued Dividend Growth Stocks

Regardless of the market, traders can find value by discovering profitable trades. So, how would you go out and find underestimated dividend stocks? We LOVE dividend growth stocks due to their share price upside potential. The strategy of investing in dividend growth stocks is an ideal approach to generate value in the form of the price appreciation along with getting a steady stream of income.

I love to buy dividend growth stocks at a reasonable price. I utilized the following strategy to buy Target Corporation at a +5% yield. We also obtained Boeing stock at $129.11 per share and the stock is currently exchanging at $344.25.

Utilize our dividend growth stock screener criteria below, and you can enhance the returns in your portfolio. My stock screening process will help you to generate maximum returns. This is where FINVIZ has been extremely helpful to use.

4.2. Dividend Growth at a Reasonable Price (dGARP)

When discovering undervalued dividend growth stocks, I get a kick out of the chance to consider it the dGARP strategy. The dGARP technique signifies "Profit Growth at a Reasonable Price." Finding Dividend Growth at a Reasonable Price (dGARP) is a procedure that consolidates precepts of both an expectation of increasing dividends over time at an attractive valuation

Usually, traditional investors consider stocks by looking at their earnings potential. However, I also prefer to find stocks that have fair valuations. Utilizing our dividend growth screener and criteria, I trust we can discover a rundown of underestimated dividend growth stocks.

Investing in undervalued stocks is the best way to amplify your aggregate return. You actually get paid (through profit pay) to hold up until the point when the valuation has achieved a market price.

In any case, discovering undervalued stocks isn't always straightforward so you should have the best possible criteria set up from the beginning.

What criteria should I use to screen for undervalued dividend growth stocks?

Using different online stock screeners, you can easily filter for stocks that have specific dividend yields, earnings growth potential, valuation, and much more.

Once you navigate to the stock screener, use the following criteria to find undervalued dividend growth stocks:

   a. Consider dividend stocks with yield greater than 0%.
   b. Market Capitalization should be over $10bln.
   c. Input price to earnings ratio below 20x.
   d. Earnings per share must be higher than 5%.
   e. PEG ratio of dividend stock should stand around 1.

Here are the means by which to gauge the dividend growth rate for the following years. This is likewise a standout amongst the most vital criteria in screening for undervalued dividend stocks since we are looking to discover stocks that consolidate the dividend growth and share price appreciation.

The Price to Earnings Growth method is commonly utilized for Growth at Reasonable Price (GARP) traders.

Dividend investors are suggested to look closely at the payout ratio if they want a safety over the long term. Analysts recommend buying companies that are offering a payout ratio in the range of 50%. On the off chance that EPS doesn't develop, there is enough room for the company to sustain their dividends.

Here is an infographic that will help you screen for undervalued dividend growth stocks:

FINDING UNDERVALUED DIVIDEND GROWTH STOCKS

Market capitalization of over $10 BILLION. I only want companies with scale and a size advantage.

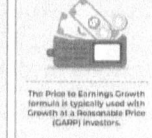

The Price to Earnings Growth formula is typically used with Growth at a Reasonable Price (GARP) investors.

We only want reasonably valued companies, so input P/E ratio **LESS THAN 20X.**

Long-term growth is important, so filter companies that are growing their EPS over the long-term. I input EPS growth next 5 years of **GREATER THAN 5%.**

I don't like to overpay for growth, so input Price to Earnings Growth ("PEG") of **LESS THAN 1.**

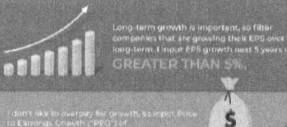

This is one of the most uncertain criteria because the growth component is highly subjective. Here's how to forecast the **DIVIDEND GROWTH RATE.**

At the same time, this is also one of the most important criteria in screening for undervalued dividend growth stocks because we are trying to find stocks that combine both dividends and **GROWTH POTENTIAL AT A REASONABLE PRICE.**

Finally, I want dividend safety over the long-term. I use a payout ratio of **LESS THAN 50%.** This gives us a margin of safety. If EPS doesn't grow, there is still sufficient dividend coverage.

INPUT DIVIDEND YIELD STOCKS GREATER THAN 0%. We only want stocks that pay a dividend.

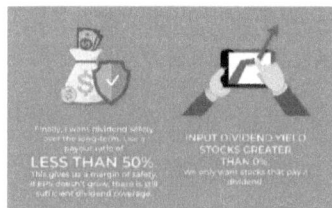

> "If investing is entertaining, if you're having fun, you're probably not making any money. Good investing is boring."
>
> —George Soros

MILLIONAIRE MOB   www.MillionaireMob.com

4.3. How to Screen for Undervalued Dividend Growth Stocks

It's a wise strategy to screen stocks and receive economic alerts to regularly review the valuations. With the technological innovations and increasing trading platforms, traders can now easily automate their investing process. By utilizing distinctive stock screeners, you position yourself for higher achievement in stock market trading. Likewise, this gives you comfort that the stocks you are putting resources into are meeting YOUR specific criteria.

It's incredible to have a rundown of stocks to look over. How would you interpret the outcomes from your stock screener?

After you input the majority of the criteria recognized above, you ought to have a rundown of stocks close to 20-40 dividend stocks to assess further.

I like to review stocks that have a lower Price-to-Earnings ratio. Keep in mind, a low Price-to-Earnings ratio does not constantly mean higher returns. Several stocks with low Price-to-Earnings ratios are foreseen to have declining earnings growth.

When you have your list of screened dividend stocks, filer the list to choose the best among them.

4.4. Compare Dividend Growth Screener Results with Dividend Aristocrats Index

To take it one step further, think about your list of screened stocks with the dividend aristocrats index. Dividend aristocrats are companies that have paid dividends over the last 25 consecutive years. In the event that you need to make it a stride further, you can compare your screened stocks with dividend kings. Dividend Kings are stocks that have been expanding their dividends for 50 successive years.

On the off chance that you like to not put resources into single dividend stocks, traders can create a portfolio of several dividend stocks.

Screening and selecting stocks for your dividend portfolio is just the first step. You are not done yet. Traders need to look at many other aspects of the stocks such as cash flow generation potential and future fundamentals to get a better idea of the bigger picture.

Chapter 5: Dividend Discount Model

5.1. What is the Dividend Discount Model?

The dividend discount model (DDM) is a method for esteeming a stock's price by discounting down anticipated dividends to the present value. On the off chance that the value obtained from the DDM is higher than the present exchanging stock price, then the stock is underestimated.

$$\text{Value of Stock} = \frac{\text{Dividend per share}}{\text{Discount Rate} - \text{Dividend growth rate}}$$

The dividend discount model depends on the possibility that the characteristic estimation of a stock can be evaluated by the anticipated estimation of the cash flows it will create later on. The driving standard behind the model is the net present value (NPV) of the cash flows, which draws from the idea of the time value of money (TVM).

5.2. Short-Form Dividend Discount Model

The short-form of the dividend discount model just takes a multiple of pro forma dividend payments. It unquestionably has its restriction in viable utilization. However, it can be utilized as a fair gauge to tell you to keep diving into the dividend growth stock further.

For predicting your future dividend growth rate, don't simply utilize one year of chronicled profit development rate. I would propose taking something like 5-year normal at the very least. Keep in mind, chronicled results are not the guarantee of future execution. Take it with a grain of salt since it is more of a craft than a science.

5.3. Multi-Stage Dividend Discount Model

The equity valuation method which is created on the idea of the Gordon Growth Model is called the multistage dividend discount model. Under the multistage model, changing development rates are connected to various eras. Different renditions of the multistage model exist including the two-stage, H, and three-stage models.

5.4. Problems with Using the Dividend Discount Model

Disadvantages of utilizing the dividend discount model (DDM) include the trouble of precise projections because it doesn't factor in buybacks.

The DDM doles out an incentive to stock by basically utilizing a sort of discounted cash flow (DCF) investigation to decide the present estimation of future anticipated dividends. On the off chance that the value decided is higher than the stock's present share price, then the stock is thought to be underestimated and worth purchasing.

While the DDM can be useful in assessing potential dividends from a stock, it has a few inalienable disadvantages. The first is that it can't be utilized to assess stocks that don't pay dividends, paying little mind to the capital allocations related to reinvesting into the business. The DDM is based on the imperfect presumption that the main estimation of a stock is the return on investment it gives through dividends.

Another shortcoming of the DDM is that, for the value calculation, it uses a number of assumptions including growth rates and required rate of returns. Dividend yields can change substantially over time. If any of the projections or assumptions made in the calculation is even slightly in error, this can result in an analyst determining a value for a stock that is significantly off in terms of being overvalued or undervalued. There are a number of variations of the DDM that attempt to overcome this problem. However, most of them involve making additional projections and calculations that are also subject to errors that are magnified over time.

5.5. What Is the Gordon Growth Model or Short-Form Dividend Discount Model?

The Gordon Growth Model explains the present estimation of a vast arrangement of future dividends. These dividends are accepted to develop at a steady rate in the future. Given the model's effortlessness, it is by and large utilized for organizations with stable growth rates; for example, blue chip organizations. These organizations are settled and reliably pay profits to their investors at a consistent pace, given their relentless money streams.

The model was named in the 1960s after Professor Myron J. Gordon, but Gordon was not the only financial scholar to popularize the model. In the 1930s, Robert F. Weise and John Burr Williams also produced significant work in this area. There are two forms of the model: the short-form (stable) model and the multistage dividend growth model. For our analysis, we will only focus on the stable (short-form) dividend discount model. The DDM is a great way to get a gut check on a dividend stock.

Dividend Discount Model Formula (Gordon Growth Model)

Value of a Stock = Next Year's Expected Annual Dividend Per Share / (Rate of Return – Expected Dividend Growth Rate)

The value of a stock equals next year's expected annual dividend per share divided by the difference between rates of return and the expected dividend growth rate. By doing this calculation, you are essentially using a multiple on next year's dividend per share. This is similar to a **capitalization rate** and assumes these rates happen into perpetuity.

Here is the true definition of the Gordon Growth Model:

Value of **stock** = $D_1 / (k - g)$
where:
D_1 = next year's expected annual dividend per share
k = the investor's discount rate or required rate of return, which can be estimated using the Capital Asset Pricing Model or the Dividend Growth Model (see Cost of Equity)
g = the expected dividend growth rate (note that this is assumed to be constant)

For inputting your future growth rate, do not just use one year of historical dividend growth rate. I would suggest taking at least a 5-year average at a minimum. Remember, historical results are not representative of future performance. Take it with a grain of salt since it is a bit more of an art than a science. Forecasting the dividend growth rate is the most important input into the model.

Download my <u>dividend discount model</u> and try valuing a few stocks on your own.

Chapter 6: Dividend Growth Rate Forecast Methods

6.1. How to Forecast the Dividend Growth Rate?

The dividend growth rate is the annualized rate of development that a specific stock experiences over some undefined time frame. The dividend growth rate is fundamental for utilizing the dividend discount model.

The stable dividend growth from any company could indicate the future growth is highly expected. At the point when an individual ascertains the dividend expansion rate, they can utilize any data from its history. They may also ascertain the dividend development rate utilizing the least squares technique or by taking a straightforward annualized figure overtime frame.

It's good to create a specific set of rules to establish the qualitative characteristics of your dividend growth rate forecast. For instance, you can create the following rules to gauge the future dividend expansion rate:

a) The expected earnings growth for the next year.
b) Check out the payout ratio to see whether the company has the potential to sustain the payout ratio over the long-term.
c) Future fundamentals of the company's business
d) The industry outlook is important.

Traders can also use a two-stage dividend growth model instead of the dividend discount model to examine the future dividend hikes. However, if you are looking for a quick and dirty analysis, you can use the short-form dividend discount model.

6.2. What Other Considerations Are Needed for Dividend Growth Investing?

It's not a wise strategy to only look at the dividend yield to determine the dividend growth stock for your portfolio. The dividend yield is solely dependent on the movement of the share price. When shares move higher, the dividend yield moves down, and when the share price declines the dividend yield goes higher. Below are the few metrics that investors should analyze for examining the dividend growth potential of any stock:

a. Free cash flow
b. Financial health
c. Management team
d. Reputation in the industry
e. Do you understand the business model?

6.3. Expert Opinion on How to Forecast Dividend Growth Rate

Portfolio manager Craig Jerusalim of Canadian equities at CIBC Global Asset Management says, "A company with a high yield does not translate to a good company, nor a safe investment."

The portfolio manager warns investors that a large downside price movement could have the potential to wipe out the long dividend history of any company. For instance, General Electric has recently reduced its dividend by half after paying solid dividends in the last decade. That's why the portfolio manager believes in dividend sustainability and the potential growth opportunity instead of higher yields and a long dividend history.

Energy companies are among the biggest examples of this. These companies usually offer higher dividend yields. However, their dividend sustainability potential is quite low because of their business models and significant dependence on commodity prices. After paying a significant dividend from 2010 to 2015, the majority of energy companies listed in the New York Stock Exchange had slashed their dividends by half in 2016. This is due to a huge downside movement in commodity prices.

"There are two indicators to look at when determining whether a company's dividends have growth potential and are sustainable," says Jerusalim. These two indicators include:

a) The flexibility of a low payout ratio.
b) Whether a company has a return on capital that exceeds its cost of capital.

Overall, it's not wise to rely on dividend yields alone. Investors should look at several other factors to achieve maximum returns from your investment.

Chapter 7: The Role of Technical Analysis in Stock Selection

7.1. The Importance of Technical Analysis

Technical analysis is very important as several technical indicators can accurately pick the future performance of a stock's price. Investors can make technical analysis of any instrument; whose price movement is dependent on supply and demand forces. Stock, bond, currency pairs, indices, and other securities performance are highly dependent on the supply and demand factors.

Analysts and investors have developed several technical indicators to gauge future performances. Every indicator has its own importance, according to the market trends and price movements. A few of them are significantly focused on predicting the existing market trends. Some of the popular current market indicators are resistance and support areas. On the other hand, the technical analysis also helps in determining the potential movements in prices.

Compared to fundamental analysis, technical analysis is a bit of a difficult job. It involves several mathematical figures and trading techniques. However, identifying trends is vital when buying stocks for the dividend portfolio. The question is, *how do investors spot a trend?* It's tricky, as the stock market doesn't consist of a group of few peoples, while the market sentiments never move in a straight line. For instance, it's not compulsory that a stock that falls in the last few days will be rebounding in the future.

According to the technical research, "lower highs and lower lows mean a downtrend and generally higher highs and higher lows indicate an uptrend."

However, sometimes it's easy to spot trends. For instance, when the U.S. dollar increases, traders can expect a downward trend in commodities and precious metals. On the hand, when the dollar declines, there is a high chance of an upward trend for safe haven assets. To spot the trend, it's necessary to look at the market indicators and stock-related news.

A trend usually shows the sentiments of traders, and trends can differ in duration from small to in-between, to long term.

Analysts and investors always prefer to trade with trends and trading against the trends can be risky. Technical analysis is extensively used in trend trading, including both technical indicators and chart patterns. Investors use several indicators and charts to spot trends.

7.2. The Importance of Moving Average and How to Use a Moving Average to Buy Stocks

The moving average (MA) is a straightforward specialized examination instrument that helps indicate the price movement by looking at the average price. Traders can take an average of any specific time frame from 10 minutes or 30 weeks to several months. There are many advantages attached to using moving averages and investors have the options to use different types of moving averages.

7.3. Why Use a Moving Average?

Moving averages can help investors to straightforwardly predict where the price of the stock is going, helping to cut the clatter on a share price chart. If the average price is angled up, this means the price is generally moving up, while angled down means the price is going down. Sideways trends suggest the share price is range-bound.

The moving average is important in technical analysis, as MA can also behave as resistance and support. In an uptrend, a 20 days, 50 days, or 200 days, moving averages have the potential to operate as a support level. On the other hand, moving averages can also have the potential act as a resistance.

Normally, if the share price of any stock is rising above the moving average, there is an upward trend. If the price is trading below the moving average, this indicates a downward trend.

7.4. Types of Moving Averages

There are several ways to calculate moving averages. For instance, a five-day simple moving average (SMA) uses the closing price of the last five days and then divides it by 5 to get a new average each day.

The exponential moving average (EMA) is one of the more well-liked types of moving averages used to predict the stock trend. Although calculating EMA can be a little complex, it essentially creates more weighting to the latest prices. EMA 50 days moving average reacts more rapidly compared to SMA 50-day moving average. Investors don't need to get involved in calculating moving averages, as there are several types of software in the market to calculate them for you.

One type of MA isn't better than another. An EMA may work better in a stock or financial market for a time, and at other times an SMA may work better. The time frame chosen for a moving average will also play a significant role in how effective it is (regardless of type).

There are numerous ways to use moving averages, including crossovers. You will get a buy signal after 50-day crosses above the 200-day. On the contrary, you will get a sell signal if 50-day declines below the 200-day.

The 20-day moving average is also beneficial for a shorter-term trader, as this moving average pursues the stock price more strongly.

Historical stock price data is always utilized to get moving averages. Thus, investors should expect more random results when using moving averages. Although, sometimes market pundits give so much importance to moving averages and signals originating from these averages, while sometimes market participants show no respect for trends coming from moving averages.

One major problem is if the price action becomes choppy, the price may swing back and forth generating multiple trends, reversal/trade signals. When this occurs, it's best to step aside or utilize another indicator to help clarify the trend.

One noteworthy issue is that if the value activity winds up plainly uneven, the stock price may swing forward and backward producing various pattern inversion/exchange signals. At the point when this happens, it's best to move to one side or use another indicator to help illuminate the pattern. In strong trending conditions, MA's work really well, but expect low results in choppy or ranging conditions.

7.5. Candlestick Patterns

In order to see the price data for various times into a single bar, there is no better way than Candlestick charts. These are considerably valuable compared to traditional simple lines that connect the dots of closing prices and open-high, low-close bars (OHLC). Moreover, strong color coding helps to create better Candlestick patterns.

Candle body is used to form a Candlesticks charts. Candle body represents the area between the open and close price, while wicks represent the high and low. When a solid candle body is formed, this is considered to be an open low and the close high. When the candle appears to have a less solid body, it shows that the stock price is volatile and is range-bound. Candles are always helpful in predicting the sentiments of the markets and future price movement. Candlesticks can also give clues to price action and the mood of the market towards a certain stock or index.

Let's discuss few important candlestick patterns in detail:

Bullish Engulfing Candlestick Pattern

A bullish engulfing candle pattern is easy to detect. When a bullish engulfing candle pattern occurs, analysts suggest that investors should buy stocks, as the price is likely to move higher. This pattern shows the price has hit the bottom, found the support it needs, and is set to rebound.

Let's take the example of Chevron to see how accurate the bullish engulfing pattern is. As shown in the above chart, in December of 2012, Chevron Corporation's (CVX) stock price formed a bullish engulfing pattern. The stock moved upwards sharply after hitting the lows and finding support at $106 a share.

Bearish Engulfing Candlestick
On the other hand, a bearish engulfing candlestick pattern is the inverse of bullish engulfing candlesticks. When this pattern occurs, analysts expect prices to move down. This type of pattern usually occurs when the stock price trades at the highest levels.

Goldman Sachs' share price hit the highest level of $129 a share in March of 2012 and, at that point, a bearish engulfing candlestick pattern occurred, and the price moved down significantly in the following months.

Three Line Strike

Although, its name suggests a three-line strike, the Bullish Three Line Strike holds four candles. Investors consider three of the four as "strikes." However, when following the three-candle upward trend, a fourth candle moves down.

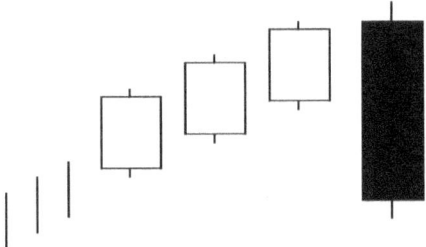

To understand the pattern, there must be an uptrend and a green or white candle must also appear on the first day. Similar types of candles also must appear on the second and third day and show the uptrend. These candles show that the price is moving higher. After these three upward candles, a black (or red) candle, which opens higher than the previous candles but then dips down, closing below the first candle's opening price. In the end, this fourth candle should contain the real bodies of the three previous candles within its length.

Two Black Gapping

When the stock price of any company hits its highest level, the bearish two black gapping continuation patterns appears. This pattern appears with a gap down that yields two black bars posting lower lows. This is an indication that the stock price will decline further from lower lows, perhaps significantly downwards.

Three Black Crows

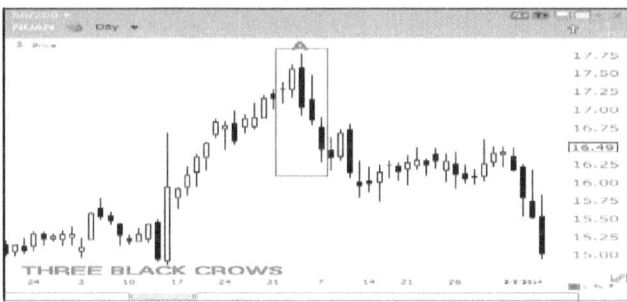

The three black crows pattern is a bearish trend which helps investors to avoid significant losses. This pattern occurs when the stock price hits the highest level with three black bars posting lower lows that close near intrabar lows. This movement of the share price shows that the price is likely to make a big downward trend.

Evening Star

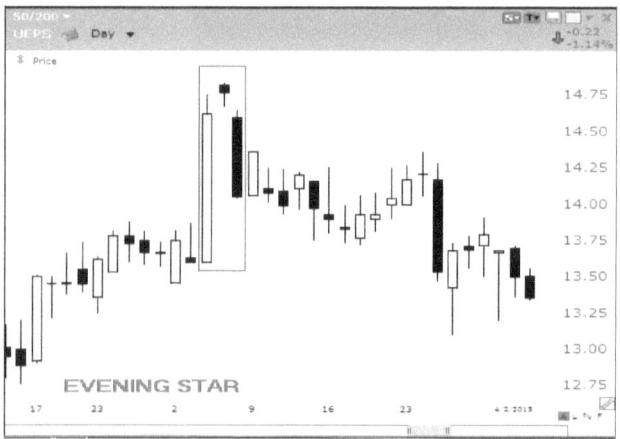

When a white tall candle appears on the chart, it could be an indication of the bearish evening star reversal pattern. The price of the stock should also increase the next day from the previous day and then a gap down on the third bar completes the pattern, predicting an even further decline from lower lows.

Abandoned Baby

At the low of any downtrend, the bullish abandoned baby reversal pattern is likely to occur. This pattern occurs when a sequence of black candles appears in a downward trend. This pattern has the potential to predict that the price will move sharply higher after hitting lowest level. This indicator is important to understand as this could lead investors to buy stock on dips with the potential to move higher in the days to come.

Chapter 8: How to Improve Income Through Smart Strategies

8.1. How to Pick a Technically and Fundamentally Sound Stock for Dividend Portfolio

When an investor decides to buy a dividend stock, he should look at several different aspects. In the discussion above, we have explicitly discussed various factors for dividend investing and we have also outlined fundamental and technical aspects of dividend investing.

Let's draw two examples: In the first case, we will discuss why Caterpillar is a solid pick for dividend investors. The second case will discuss why General Electric is a poor buy for dividend investors.

Caterpillar Is a Great Dividend Stock

Caterpillar is among those companies that have extensive dividend history and large business models. Caterpillar's revenue and cash generation potential is also strong enough to support dividends. In addition, its payout ratio is standing in the range of 30% to 40% of income, which is considered a perfect payout ratio for dividend investors. Caterpillar has paid higher dividends to its shareholders over more than 20 consecutive years and, since 2007, the company's cash dividend has more than doubled. Caterpillar has paid a cash dividend every year since the company was formed and has paid a quarterly dividend since 1933.

Therefore, investors can pick Caterpillar for their dividend stock portfolio. But it's also important for investors to choose the right time to enter into a company. If an investor buys a stock at 52-weeks high, this couldn't help him in generating higher gains from share price appreciation, though he would be entitled to big dividends.

Buying companies on the dip with strong future fundamentals is always deemed as a perfect trading strategy. Caterpillar is among those companies that have strong market presence in global markets and its brand recognition and technological innovations continue to help it in extending the market share.

Why Isn't General Electric a Good Buy for Dividend Investors?

The dip in share price is not always a buying opportunity. In addition, strong future fundamentals are very important for the stock to keep the uptrend. General Electric has presented two perfect examples for dividend investors. Its stock price increased steadily in 2016, as the company started restructuring its business model and the management presented a rosy picture for the future.

However, advanced investors with a strong understanding of industrial businesses knew that the company would take a much longer time to move their business model from financial services to industrial business. Thus, they were expecting its share price to plunge but investors with less understanding of future fundamentals were easily fooled by the rosy presentations from the management.

In the beginning of 2017, investors started to realize that the restructuring process would take a longer time and the company would need massive cash inflows to support the change. Thus, GE's share price started to decline. But, in this case, the dip in its share price didn't indicate the perfect buying opportunity as its cash flow position and lower earning potential were creating difficulties for the company to sustain its dividend. Therefore, the company recently announced to slash its dividends by 50%.

Candlestick chart patterns and moving averages were also presenting the downward trend in its share price since the start of this year. More than one bearish Engulfing Candlestick pattern appeared on its chart in the last eleven months. GE isn't presenting a buying opportunity despite the massive selloff. The company's future fundamentals are bleak, and its cash position isn't strong enough to support dividends and restructuring actions. The company needs to make several acquisitions to expand its presence in the industrial businesses.

8.2. Income Generation Through Binary Trading

The U.S. stock market has been moving on up since the 2009 financial crisis. But there is no guarantee that the markets will continue to move higher over the long-term. Investors should structure their portfolios more towards high-income generation rather than growth.

Covered calls are among the best way to generate income. The covered call options trading strategy is generally easy to understand. Analysts believe that when one combines covered calls with dividend stocks, the result would be impressive.

Although option trading is a bit risky for defensive investors, covered calls are a great way to get started with options. There is a natural progression for an investor who is already accustomed to share ownership to begin to explore the fabulous world of covered calls. Investors only need to educate themselves which requires a lot of practice.

Covered calls are among the best wealth formation tools. This is because a covered call protects an investor's downside risk on investment and it helps investors to earn additional income.

8.3. What Are Covered Calls?

Covered calls are an options strategy where a trader holds a long position in a stock and writes (offers) the same asset to create income. This is frequently utilized when an income investor believes that the stock is likely to make small movements in the short-term. The investor simultaneously has a short position in that asset in the form of an option to generate some income from a premium he or she is expecting to receive from exercising that option.

However, this strategy doesn't work strongly for bullish investors. The covered call works as a hedge on long positions and it permits investors to generate income in the form of a premium received from writing the option.

The covered call option works well for the bearish investor as this strategy allows investors to generate income and helps to offset the loss on the stock if it should plummet.

8.4. Example of Writing Covered Calls with Dividend Growth Stocks

Let's look at an example to clearly understand how a covered call option works in boosting returns:

ABC stock is trading at almost $100 a share and you believe the stock doesn't have the potential to make a meaningful upside in the days to come. In that case, an investor is looking to boost his income by using the covered call option with a strike price of $100.

On the other hand, the buyer of the option is bullish on the stock and he believes the price will move higher in the coming days. For the right to buy the stock for $100, the option buyer pays you a premium of $5.

Let's look at some scenarios…

Scenario #1: Stock goes to $85

If the stock declines to $85, the buyer of the option would lose his entire investment of $5. You still hold the stock, but you are likely to lose $10 instead of $15.

Scenario #2: Stock stays at $100

If the stock price continues trading close to $100, the buyer will lose all investment. In that case, the holder of the stock will get $5 return despite a sideways movement.

Stock goes to $105

If the stock price moves to $105, the buyer of the option could sell the shares in the open market to make a $5 return. However, the buyer's profit will be zero as the buyer paid $5 for the option.

Stock goes to $115

If the stock price increases to $115, both investors are likely to take advantage of the price hike. The seller will make $5 and the buyer will also be happy purchasing shares at $100 of the stock that is now trading around $115.

Investor Returns		
Stock Price	Option Buyer	Stock Owner
$85	($5.00)	($10.00)
$90	($5.00)	($5.00)
$95	($5.00)	$0.00
$100	($5.00)	$5.00
$105	$0.00	$5.00
$110	$5.00	$5.00
$115	$10.00	$5.00
$120	$15.00	$5.00

Example of call buyer returns

8.5. Best Stocks for Covered Call Writing

Here are the best stocks for writing calls:

a) Dividend stocks are best for covered call writing.
b) Exercising covered calls on overvalued stocks is a good strategy.

c) Using covered call options on any significant event could also help investors in mitigating losses.

Although options trading carries a lot of risk for new investors, the trading strategy could also help in accumulating big gains in the short-term. Option trading not only offers bigger returns to investors, it also provides higher cost efficiency. Options trading also allows investors to make upside, downside, and sideways.

8.6. What Are Put Options?

Put options are financial contracts giving the owner the right, but not the obligation, to sell a specified amount of an underlying security at a specified price within a specified time frame.

Put options are worth considering as they allow investors to trim down the risk by setting a predefined contract at a specified price to sell. The put option works as a hedge for investors, allowing them to sell the stock at a specified price before it goes down.

The value of the put option declines with passage of time as the possibility of stock price declining below the strike price reduces.

8.7. Writing Puts for Income Checklist

Weekly put options are contracts that expire on a weekly basis. These options are less expensive and ensure big gains if an investor uses the proper strategies.

8.8. What Are the Stock Long-Term Fundamentals?

Investors should closely gauge the market fundamentals before making any investment in dividend stocks. The market fundamentals clearly suggest where the stock price is moving in the long haul despite volatile movement in the short-term.

Market fundamentals indicate the outlook of the overall environment of the end markets in which the company is operating.

Market fundamentals are key when you are trading put options. For instance, if the stock falls due to some unfortunate event, traders can easily judge the future movement if they have a keen eye of future fundamentals.

Additionally, traders need to look at the broader market environment between the time they execute the put option sale and its expiration.

8.9. What Are Material Events Happening Between Now and Expiration of the Weekly Put Option?

Investors need to be aware of any upcoming event that could have a meaningful impact on a stock's price. Material events can include economic reports, earnings releases, monthly sales reports, etc.

Some traders like to write weekly puts on stocks that they already own since they know the stock is fundamentally strong and they understand the fluctuations on a daily/weekly basis. On the other hand, if you don't have enough knowledge about the stock's fundamentals, you should look at the charts to understand how the stock reacts to certain headline events.

Chapter 9: Which Sectors Offer Best Dividends?

9.1. Where to Look for Dividend Stocks

Investors usually think that there are only two major sectors, including Telecom and Utilities, offering higher and more stable dividends. There is no doubt these two sectors have been paying significant dividend yields and they have sustained their dividend yields over the past ten years. The average yield in the Telecom industry stands at 4.8%, while utilities average dividend yield is close to 3.5%.

The Utilities sector is composed of several industries such as gas, electricity, and water utilities. These industries are usually considered as safe havens for investors, as the barrier to entry in these industries is very high, creating a competitive advantage for the existing players. The consumer demand has always been increasing at a steady rate, thanks to the nature of their products. We cannot live without water, electricity, and gas and there is no alternative to these products. Therefore, these companies have the potential to generate a sustainable growth over the long-term.

There are more than 13 utility companies that are standing on the list of dividend aristocrats. For instance, Consolidated Edison, Inc. (ED) and American States Water Co (AWR) are among those companies that have increased their dividends in the last 25 straight years.

On the other hand, Telecom industry has experienced a significant boost in the last ten years, supported by massive technological innovations. The telecom industry has players like AT&T (T) and Verizon (VZ), which both offer dividend yields close to 5%. These companies have a proven track record of rewarding shareholders through dividends. At the moment, their cash generation is both stable and predictable.

After the slump of 2007/08, investors moved towards high dividend stocks to use them as a hedge against economic downturns. This is the major reason behind the popularity of the telecom and utilities sectors.

However, investors shouldn't stick to these two sectors alone. There are many other sectors that offer significant cash returns to investors.

The Technology sector, for example, is among the booming sectors in the stock market. This sector is extensive and includes industries like IT services, semiconductor manufacturing, telecommunications, software, biotechnology, data hosting services, and scientific research. The average dividend yield for this sector is just over 3%. The number of dividend paying companies has been increasing at a significant rate. In 2003, there were only 22 dividend stocks, but the number of dividend paying companies is now above 50.

Technology accounts for almost 15% of all dividends paid, but this sector tops the list when it comes to measuring the number of dividends paid on a dollar basis. Over the last couple of years, the technology sector has generated massive growth. Companies like Facebook (FB), Google (GOOG), NVIDIA (NVDA), Cisco (CSCO), Microsoft (MSFT) and others are generating considerable growth in sales and earnings. Thus, they have also been returning significant dividends to investors.

Consumer discretionary stocks and Financial Companies have also seen a notable growth in dividends. Investors had invested substantially in the consumer staple sectors due to their stable cash generation potential. However, higher investments in these companies boosted their stock's prices, making them overvalued.

The consumer discretionary sector includes all those companies whose products are purchased by consumers instead of businesses and manufacturers. These companies sell products ranging from food products to apparel to paper products and auto parts. This sector is highly dependent on consumer spending and economic environment.

This sector has a high price to earnings ratio, standing close to 22 times– the highest level in the last ten years.

The consumer discretionary sector has an average dividend yield of 2.22%. Tobacco is the highest yielding industry in this sector. This sector has more than 21 companies that have increased dividend in the last 25 straight years such as Kimberly Clark (KMB), Altria (MO), and Pepsico (PEP). Income investors can also find several other new companies in the sectors that are offering higher cash returns to investors. These companies also have the potential to generate big dividend growth and price appreciation.

Stable earnings potential from telecom, utilities, and consumer staples is the major reason behind their successful dividend history. These companies have the potential to generate strong earnings in any environment, as consumers aren't going to give up their Internet, shut off their power, or stop buying toothpaste when the market is under depression.

A few sectors in the stock market, for example, Basic materials, additionally pay higher dividends, but there is also a bigger risk attached to these companies.

These companies generally have to invest significantly in future growth opportunities. In addition, their business models are highly correlated to commodity prices. Thus, these businesses are a place for investors who can take a high risk. For instance, energy and mining companies had paid a massive dividend between 2010 to 2014, but they slashed their dividend payouts by more than 50% in 2016, due to their significant dependence on commodity prices.

A great portfolio ought to have a blend of high-yielding organizations and lower-paying, growth-oriented names. The objective, however, is to hold a bushel of stocks that compensate for more than the S&P 500's.

You have to adopt a multidimensional strategy and not simply concentrate on the most astounding profit paying areas. Develop a portfolio with some appealing organizations that have low or no profits and balance that by putting resources into organizations with higher yields. The total portfolio ought to have a greater yield than the market.

Here is an infographic on how you should think about building a dividend portfolio.

BUILDING AN OPTIMAL DIVIDEND GROWTH PORTFOLIO?

You need proper diversification. Thus, limiting overlapping industries and having balanced allocations among your holdings is key.

I suggest the following allocation exposures to different types of dividend stocks to create a successful dividend growth portfolio:

 20% of your dividend portfolio should be allocated to Dividend Kings.

 35% of your dividend growth portfolio should be allocated to Dividend Aristocrats.

30% of your dividend portfolio should be allocated to up and coming dividend stocks.

We want stocks that have demonstrated a track record of increasing their dividend and rewarding shareholders,

but are not considered the 'classic' dividend growth stocks like the Dividend Kings or Dividend Aristocrats.

The remaining 15%

of your asset allocation in your dividend growth portfolio should be international dividend growth stocks.

You can get a basket of international dividend growth stocks by investing in an global dividend growth fund. Or, you can select individual blue chip international dividend growth stocks. I suggest investing in a global dividend growth fund to get the best outcome and the broadest exposure of diversification.

Keep in mind Dividend Aristocrats have a strong track record of success.

Dividend Kings are likely slower growers, but have an even better track record of success.

I like to invest in Dividend Kings at reasonable valuations. View our list of all of the Dividend Kings at the bottom of the page.

Great

These percentages help, but how many stocks should I have?

I think you should have about 30 distinct stocks in your dividend portfolio.

There are a lot of good dividend stocks out there, so you want to broaden your exposure and reduce your risk.

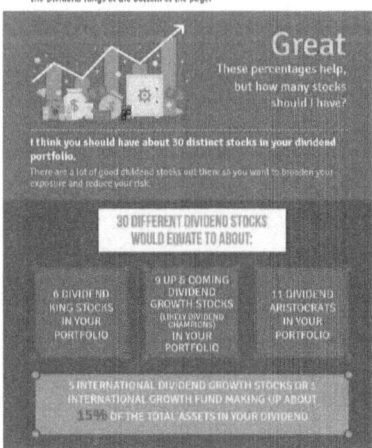

30 DIFFERENT DIVIDEND STOCKS WOULD EQUATE TO ABOUT:

- **6 DIVIDEND KING STOCKS IN YOUR PORTFOLIO**
- **9 UP & COMING DIVIDEND GROWTH STOCKS (LIKELY DIVIDEND CHAMPIONS) IN YOUR PORTFOLIO**
- **11 DIVIDEND ARISTOCRATS IN YOUR PORTFOLIO**

5 INTERNATIONAL DIVIDEND GROWTH STOCKS OR 1 INTERNATIONAL GROWTH FUND MAKING UP ABOUT 15% OF THE TOTAL ASSETS IN YOUR DIVIDEND

Chapter 10: The Theoretical Case Against Dividend Investing

Regardless of their relative investment thesis for dividend investing, an investor shouldn't accept the fact that a high dividend yield stock is going to be risk-free and always offer higher return to investors. Investors need to be cautious while picking high dividend yielding stocks.

In some cases, the dividend yield of few companies soars massively. This does not necessarily mean the company is offering hefty returns to investors. In these cases, the dividend yield of the company increases only due the drop in the stock price. The share price of the company drops when investors think the company has bleak future fundamentals. Thus, higher dividend yields can be a warning sign that the company is going to face a big disaster.

Investors should do a lot of research before picking any dividend stock. For instance, the ABC Company offers a dividend yield of more than 7% to investors, but the higher dividend yield is only due to the drop of nearly 50% in its share price, which pushed it dividend yield from 3.5% to 7%. The company sales growth and earnings are in trouble and the company is looking for ways to expand these figures. They could move towards acquisitions to support the revenue and earnings growth, which could eventually reduce their potential to support dividends. Thus, there is a big chance of dividend cut.

In spite of the plenty of experimental confirmation, in principle, financial specialists ought to be apathetic in the matter of whether free cash flows are paid out by means of dividend or reinvested in the organization. We can comprehend this idea from both the organization's point of view and the financial specialist's standpoint. According to the company standpoint, dividend growth or reduction can be made by making adjustments in the capital investments. For instance, companies can expand their dividends by issuing new stock, but this would impact the existing shareholders; a higher number of outstanding shares will force the company to distribute profits to more investors. In addition, stock is typically the highest cost of capital for a company. This would be an inefficient use of capital.

However, from the investor's point of view, they can achieve divided preferences through basic portfolio transitions. Suppose an organization builds its profit yield from 2.5% to 5.0%, yet the financial specialist just needs 2.5%. He can essentially re-put the additional 2.5% into the organization, abandoning himself with an indistinguishable result if the organization had never expanded the dividend in any case.

10.1. The Case Against High Dividend Yields

High yield stocks are a poor proxy for value investing. The yield can be an intermediary for regular valuation measurements like price-to-earnings and book-to-market.

With the help of the dividend discount model, we can suppose that the stock's book value is equivalent to the net present value. With a steady development rate of dividend and consistent cost of capital, book value per stock ought to be corresponding to the present yearly dividend per share, or, comparably, book-to-market ought to be relative to dividend yield.

Likewise, if we presume dividends per share and a constant long-term payout ratio are proportional to earnings per share. The result would be the yield inversely proportional to price-to-earnings.

Several books and papers show that the high dividend yield stocks have notably smashed the broad market. Nevertheless, if we decompose the returns of the portfolio into the different factors, we will find earnings yield (earnings-to-price) and value (price-to-book) are significant contributors. Potential problems with using high yield as a value proxy are:

- o Poor growth prospects if we chase high dividend yield.
- o Chasing high dividend yield could force you to avoid profitable stocks that have for the short term reduced or suspended dividends.
- o Due to the popularity and investor's confidence, high dividend yield stocks may experience difficulties from becoming undervalued stocks compared to non-payers or lower-yielders.

Although investors see the impact of dividend and reinvestments same, in fact, they have a different impact in the long-term.

Between dividend and reinvestment, there exists a great gulf of uncertainty. A dividend today is, quite simply, not the same as a potential future return: particularly when evidence suggests that companies have historically done a terrific job of destroying reinvested capital.

Amongst reinvestment and dividend, there exists an extraordinary inlet of vulnerability. A dividend now is essentially unequal as potential future returns. This is especially the case for those organizations that have devastating reinvested capital.

Consider that companies with a high reinvestment rate have lower returns than those with a lower reinvestment rate. Let's assume that organizations with a high reinvestment rate have brought down returns compared to those companies with a lower reinvestment rate.

10.2. Dividend Growers as a Quality Proxy

It's true that companies that pay constantly increasing dividends generate better returns for investors compared to those companies that reinvest their profits back into the business. However, investors shouldn't only focus on the company's payout. They should also look at the rate of dividend growth to generate higher returns.

The management of the company has the authority to cut or increase dividends, but they'll feel strong pressure from shareholders if they cut dividends. Therefore, it is important to look for companies with friendly shareholders management.

10.3. A Note on Dividend Growth Portfolios

Like many analysts, we like companies with significant dividends for many reasons. The major reason is these companies enable investors not to follow exit strategies and they will get a steady share price appreciation along with dividends. While picking stocks, dividend growth investors need to be straightforward.

Obviously, we realize that there is no assurance that any methodology can develop profits for investors over the long-term with no interruptions, particularly during the period of recession. For instance, the S&P 500 Dividend Aristocrat Index has generated significant returns in the course of the most recent nine years, but they saw yearly profits aggregately decrease by 8.5% during 2008 to 2009. Therefore, investors should also expect losses in the case of volatile business environments or recessionary conditions.

10.4. Dividends Are Not Legally Binding

Unlike bonds, there are no legitimate repercussions for defaulting on dividend payments. Companies are not liable to pay dividends to investors. It's their discretionary power to either increase or decrease the dividend.

There is no investment strategy that comes without risks. But there is a lot of evidence to believe that dividend paying companies have generally created abundance returns. In any case, dividends may assume a vital part in helping financial specialists dodge ruinous reinvestment by organization chiefs. So, an emphasis on profit payers may enable financial specialists to catch the reinvestment premium. An attention on profit producers may permit speculators to take advantage of this premium, as well with higher quality organizations.

Conclusion

The majority of analysts believe that investors can easily outperform the overall market returns by adding high dividend stocks to their portfolio. In his book, "Beating the Dow," Michael O'Higgins discusses the 'Dogs of the Dow' strategy which attracted investors to use the yield-centered technique. He demonstrated that by putting resources into the ten most noteworthy yielding securities in the Dow Jones Industrial Average (DJIA), financial specialists could beat the market averages.

Regardless of their relative well-being, don't always accept that high dividend yield stocks are risk-free and will always offer the higher return to investors. Investors need to be cautious while picking high dividend yielding stocks. They should do both fundamentals and technical analysis of those stocks.

In some cases, the dividend yield of few companies soars massively. This does not necessarily mean the company is offering hefty returns to investors. In these cases, the dividend yield of the company increases only due to the drop in the stock price. The share price of the company drops when investors think the company has bleak future fundamentals. Thus, higher dividend yields are sometimes the warning sign that the company is going to face a big disaster.

Picking stocks only due to the high dividend yield should not be your top criteria. Investors should also look at several other matrices before diving into the dividend stock. Investors should first look at the company's dividend history to check whether it had made any dividend cuts in the past. If the company hasn't made any dividend cuts in the past, then investors should look at the dividend growth rate and how often the company raises the dividends. But relying on the history has never proved to be a wise investment strategy.

Investors should do more research on the stock. They should look at the payout ratio and the company earnings and cash flow generation potential. Generally, analysts suggest investors to pick the stocks with higher dividend yield and a low payout ratio. This is because companies with low payout ratios and high dividend yields often have more room to make dividend increases. Cash generation is very important for dividend paying companies.

If the company does not cover its capital requirements and dividend payments from its cash flows, there is a huge chance of dividend cut. The majority of dividend paying companies try to support capital investments and dividend payments through their cash flows.

If you want to achieve financial freedom through dividend investing, follow these five steps.

1. Start out by contributing $200 per month to your dividend growth portfolio
2. Increase your annual contributions by 25% each year
3. Reinvest all dividend income back into the dividend growth portfolio
4. Invest in high-quality stocks that enable you to achieve an annual 6% growth rate in your equity value
5. Rinse and repeat steps 1-4

From there you will achieve the following portfolio values as seen in my dividend calculator.

Actual $'s	Annual Contributions	Value of Portfolio1	Dividend Income2	Ending Portfolio Value		Instructions	
Year						Source: https://millionairemob.com/dividend-calculator	
0	2,400	2,400	72	2,472		1. Input Monthly Contribution	$200
1	3,000	5,724	172	5,896			
2	3,750	10,281	308	10,589		2. Input Annual Increase in Contributions	25%
3	4,688	16,481	494	16,975			
4	5,859	24,867	746	25,613		3. Assumed Annual Dividend Yield	3%
5	7,324	36,160	1,085	37,245			
6	9,155	51,317	1,540	52,856		4. Annual Capital Appreciation	6%
7	11,444	71,604	2,148	73,752			
8	14,305	98,700	2,961	101,661			
9	17,881	134,832	4,045	138,877			
10	22,352	182,951	5,489	188,439			
11	27,940	246,966	7,409	254,375			
12	34,925	332,059	9,962	342,020			
13	43,656	445,097	13,353	458,450			
14	54,570	595,179	17,855	613,035			
15	68,212	794,364	23,831	818,195			
16	85,265	1,058,630	31,759	1,090,389			
17	106,581	1,409,147	42,274	1,451,421			
18	133,227	1,873,970	56,219	1,930,189			
19	166,533	2,490,272	74,708	2,564,980			
20	208,167	3,307,307	99,219	3,406,527			

Source: MillionaireMob.com
1. Assumes a 6% growth rate per year, which is in line with long-term historical averages
2. Assumes a 3% dividend yield on your portfolio

At the end of year 20, you will earn a six-figure income and have a seven figure portfolio value. That is the power of compound interest.

Appendix: Free Resources

My goal with this book is to provide you with the best possible solutions to help you become a better investor and ultimately live completely financially free.

Here are several free downloadable resources for you to use as you consider a dividend growth investing strategy:

1. Downloadable Dividend Calculator: See what it takes to live off dividends forever. Use this calculator to input your assumptions on contributions, growth rates and dividend yield to see what it will take to replace your income with dividends.
2. Downloadable Dividend Discount Model: The dividend discount model can be used as a rough valuation for a potential dividend growth stock investment.
3. List of No-Free Dividend Reinvestment Plan Stocks: This list of all companies involved in no-free DRIP programs can help you find the appropriate stocks for automated dividend reinvestment.

www.ingramcontent.com/pod-product-compliance
Lightning Source LLC
Chambersburg PA
CBHW030506220526
45464CB00006B/2687